Employment Law and Regulations:
A Comprehensive Guide

By **Dr. R. Dominguez**

Employment Law and Regulations: A Comprehensive Guide

This book is dedicated to promoting fair and inclusive workplaces and empowering employers and employees to navigate employment law. Together, we can shape a better future of work.

Dr. R. Dominguez, IO-Psych

Content

Introduction

In today's rapidly evolving employment landscape, it is crucial for both employers and employees to have a solid understanding of the laws and regulations governing the employer-employee relationship. This comprehensive guide aims to provide you with a comprehensive overview of the intricate web of employment laws in the United States.

Understanding Employment Law Basics

Chapter 1 delves into the fundamental principles of employment law, providing you with a solid foundation upon which to explore the intricacies of this field. We begin with an overview of employment law, shedding light on its purpose and scope. Furthermore, we explore the various sources of employment law, including federal and state legislation, judicial decisions, and administrative regulations. Understanding these sources is essential for comprehending the legal framework that governs the employment relationship.

To gain insight into the practical aspects of employment law, we examine the role of government agencies responsible for enforcing and interpreting employment laws. By understanding the functions of these agencies, such as the Equal Employment Opportunity Commission (EEOC) and the Department of Labor (DOL), you will develop a comprehensive understanding of the enforcement mechanisms at play.

Part I: Laws Governing Employers and Employees

This section of the guide focuses on the laws that directly impact the employer-employee relationship. From the foundational concept of at-will employment to the exceptions that limit its application, we explore the intricacies of employment relationships in Chapter 2. Understanding the different types of employment, including at-will and contract employment, is crucial for both employers and employees to navigate their rights and obligations.

Anti-Discrimination Laws occupy a prominent place in employment law, aiming to foster equal opportunities and protect employees from unfair treatment. Chapter 3 provides an in-depth exploration of key anti-discrimination laws, such as the Civil Rights Act of 1964, the Equal Pay Act, the Age Discrimination in Employment Act, the Americans with Disabilities Act, the Pregnancy Discrimination Act, and the Genetic Information Nondiscrimination Act. By familiarizing yourself with these laws, you will gain the knowledge needed to identify and address instances of discrimination in the workplace.

Wage and Hour Laws, addressed in Chapter 4, play a crucial role in safeguarding employee rights and ensuring fair compensation. We examine the Fair Labor Standards Act (FLSA), which establishes minimum wage and overtime pay requirements, as well as exemptions from these provisions. By understanding wage and hour laws, both employers and employees can navigate the intricacies of compensation and avoid potential legal pitfalls.

Chapter 5 is dedicated to Family and Medical Leave, exploring the provisions of the Family and Medical Leave Act (FMLA). We delve into eligibility requirements, employee rights, and employer obligations when it comes to granting leave for family and medical reasons. By understanding these laws, employers can establish compliant policies, while employees can exercise their rights effectively.

Workplace Safety and Health take center stage in Chapter 6. We delve into the Occupational Safety and Health Act (OSHA) and explore the responsibilities of both employers and employees in maintaining a safe and healthy work environment. By familiarizing yourself with safety standards, inspections, and employee rights, you can promote a culture of safety and prevent workplace accidents.

Employee Benefits, examined in Chapter 7, are an essential aspect of the employment relationship. We explore laws such as the Employee Retirement Income Security Act (ERISA), the Health Insurance Portability and Accountability Act (HIPAA), the Affordable Care Act (ACA), and Employee Assistance Programs (EAPs). Understanding these laws will help both employers and employees navigate the complex landscape of employee benefits, ensuring compliance and maximizing the advantages they offer.

Part II: Government Agencies and Enforcement

In Part II, we shift our focus to the governmental bodies responsible for enforcing employment laws. Chapter 8 explores the Equal Employment Opportunity Commission (EEOC) and its role in investigating complaints of discrimination. By understanding the functions of the EEOC and the process of filing a complaint, individuals can seek redress for violations of their rights.

The Department of Labor (DOL) takes center stage in Chapter 9. We examine the Wage and Hour Division (WHD), the Occupational Safety and Health Administration (OSHA), and the Office of Federal Contract Compliance Programs (OFCCP). Understanding the responsibilities of these divisions empowers both employers and employees to ensure compliance with labor standards, safety regulations, and fair employment practices.

The National Labor Relations Board (NLRB), explored in Chapter 10, focuses on protecting employees' rights to organize, addressing unfair labor practices, and overseeing collective bargaining. By understanding the role and functions of the NLRB, employers and employees alike can navigate the complex terrain of labor relations and collective action.

Part III: Special Employment Issues

The final section of our comprehensive guide delves into special employment issues that demand particular attention. Chapter 11 examines Immigration Law and Employment, shedding light on the Immigration Reform and Control Act (IRCA) and the obligations it imposes on employers. By understanding the intricacies of immigration law, employers can ensure compliance while attracting and retaining a diverse workforce.

Privacy and Data Protection, explored in Chapter 12, is a pressing issue in the digital age. We delve into employee privacy rights, the

Electronic Communications Privacy Act (ECPA), and data breach notification laws. By understanding these legal frameworks, employers can strike a balance between utilizing technology and safeguarding employee privacy.

Chapter 13 tackles Employment Termination and Severance, covering topics such as wrongful termination, layoffs, and reductions in force, as well as the negotiation and drafting of severance agreements. Understanding these issues is crucial for both employers and employees, as navigating termination and severance processes can be legally complex and emotionally challenging.

Conclusion

In the concluding chapter of our comprehensive guide, we summarize key takeaways and provide guidance on applying the knowledge gained throughout the book. Employment law is a dynamic field, subject to continuous changes and developments. By equipping yourself with the knowledge found in this guide, you will be better prepared to navigate the ever-evolving legal landscape and make informed decisions in the realm of employee law and regulations.

Please note that while this table of contents provides a general outline, the specific focus and depth of the book may vary. We encourage readers to consult legal professionals and up-to-date sources for comprehensive and accurate information regarding employee laws and regulations in the United States.

Chapter 1: Understanding Employment Law Basics

Employment law serves as the foundation for the complex relationship between employers and employees. This chapter provides a comprehensive overview of the fundamental principles that shape the field of employment law. By understanding these basics, both employers and employees can navigate the intricacies of their rights, obligations, and legal protections in the workplace.

1.1 Overview of Employment Law:

Employment law encompasses a broad range of legal principles and regulations that govern the relationship between employers and employees. It covers areas such as hiring, compensation, working conditions, discrimination, termination, and employee benefits. The overarching goal of employment law is to ensure fair and equitable treatment in the workplace, promoting a harmonious balance between the rights and interests of employers and employees.

1.2 Sources of Employment Law:

To comprehend the legal framework of employment law, it is essential to understand its primary sources. Employment law draws from various sources, including:

a) Federal and State Legislation: The United States has a complex system of federal and state laws that regulate employment practices. At the federal level, key legislation includes the Civil Rights Act of 1964, the Fair Labor Standards Act (FLSA), the Family and Medical Leave Act (FMLA), and the Americans with Disabilities Act (ADA), among others. Additionally, each state may have its own employment laws that supplement federal regulations.

b) Judicial Decisions: Courts play a crucial role in interpreting employment laws through their decisions in legal cases. These judicial precedents establish principles and guidelines that shape the interpretation and application of employment law.

c) Administrative Regulations: Government agencies, such as the Equal Employment Opportunity Commission (EEOC) and the Department of Labor (DOL), issue regulations and guidelines that provide further clarification and implementation of employment laws. These regulations help employers and employees understand their rights and obligations more effectively.

1.3 Role of Government Agencies:

Government agencies play a vital role in the enforcement, interpretation, and administration of employment laws. Understanding the functions of these agencies is crucial for both employers and employees. Some key agencies include:

a) Equal Employment Opportunity Commission (EEOC): The EEOC is responsible for enforcing federal laws that prohibit workplace discrimination based on factors such as race, color, religion, sex, national origin, age, disability, and genetic information. It investigates complaints, facilitates settlements, and, if necessary, litigates cases on behalf of individuals who experience discrimination.

b) Department of Labor (DOL): The DOL oversees a range of employment-related issues, including wage and hour standards, workplace safety, family and medical leave, and retirement benefits. It administers and enforces laws such as the FLSA, FMLA, and ERISA, ensuring compliance and protecting the rights of workers.

c) Other Agencies: Various other government agencies focus on specific areas of employment law. For example, the Occupational Safety and Health Administration (OSHA) enforces workplace safety regulations, the Wage and Hour Division (WHD) ensures fair pay practices, and the Office of Federal Contract Compliance Programs (OFCCP) monitors equal employment opportunity requirements for federal contractors.

By understanding the functions and roles of these government agencies, both employers and employees can seek guidance, file complaints, and access resources to protect their rights and ensure compliance with employment laws.

Understanding the basics of employment law sets the stage for comprehending the rights and responsibilities of both employers and employees. By familiarizing themselves with the overview of employment law, its sources, and the role of government agencies, individuals can navigate the complex landscape of workplace regulations. It is important to note that employment law is a dynamic field, subject to changes and developments. Therefore, staying informed about updates and consulting legal professionals and up-to-date resources is crucial for comprehensive knowledge of employment law.

Part I: Laws Governing Employers and Employees

Chapter 2: Employment Relationship

The employment relationship forms the cornerstone of the employer-employee dynamic. This chapter explores the different types of employment arrangements, the concept of at-will employment, contract employment, and the exceptions that impact the nature of the employment relationship. Understanding the intricacies of these arrangements is crucial for both employers and employees to navigate their rights and obligations effectively.

2.1 At-Will Employment:

At-will employment is the most common form of employment relationship in the United States. Under this arrangement, either the employer or the employee can terminate the employment relationship at any time, for any lawful reason, or no reason at all, without incurring liability. However, certain limitations exist to safeguard against wrongful termination and protect employee rights.

2.2 Contract Employment:

Contract employment, in contrast to at-will employment, involves a legally binding agreement between the employer and employee. Contracts can be written or oral and outline specific terms and conditions of employment, such as duration, compensation, job responsibilities, and grounds for termination. Contract employment provides a greater level of job security and clarifies the rights and obligations of both parties.

2.3 Exceptions to At-Will Employment:

While at-will employment is the default standard, various exceptions have been established through legislation, court decisions, and public policy considerations. These exceptions provide additional protections for employees and restrict the employer's ability to terminate the employment relationship without cause. Some common exceptions include:

a) Implied Contracts: In some cases, an implied contract can arise, even in the absence of a written agreement. If an employer's actions or statements create an expectation of continued employment or if there is a consistent practice of progressive discipline, the courts may recognize an implied contract that limits at-will termination.

b) Public Policy Exceptions: Termination of an employee based on reasons that violate public policy is prohibited. For example, if an employee is fired for refusing to engage in illegal activities or for whistleblowing on employer misconduct, it may be considered wrongful termination.

c) Implied Covenant of Good Faith and Fair Dealing: Some states recognize an implied covenant of good faith and fair dealing, which requires employers to act in good faith and deal fairly with their employees when making employment-related decisions.

d) Statutory Protections: Certain federal and state laws protect employees from discriminatory termination based on factors such as race, gender, age, disability, national origin, religion, or protected whistleblower activities. Violations of these laws can lead to legal consequences for the employer.

Understanding these exceptions to at-will employment is essential for both employers and employees. Employers must be aware of their obligations and the potential risks associated with terminating employees, while employees can assert their rights and seek legal recourse if they believe their termination was unlawful. The employment relationship serves as the foundation for the employer-employee dynamic. Whether under the default at-will arrangement or through contract employment, understanding the intricacies of these arrangements is crucial for both employers and employees. Moreover, being aware of the exceptions to at-will employment ensures that individuals can navigate their rights and obligations effectively. By comprehending the nuances of the employment relationship, employers and employees can foster a fair and equitable workplace environment while upholding their legal responsibilities.

Chapter 3: Anti-Discrimination Laws

Promoting equal opportunities and combating discrimination is a cornerstone of employment law in the United States. This chapter delves into the essential anti-discrimination laws that protect individuals from unfair treatment based on various protected characteristics. Understanding these laws is crucial for both employers and employees to ensure a workplace free from discrimination and to foster inclusivity and diversity.

3.1 Title VII of the Civil Rights Act of 1964:

Title VII of the Civil Rights Act of 1964 is a landmark federal law that prohibits discrimination in employment on the basis of race, color, religion, sex, and national origin. Under Title VII, employers are prohibited from making decisions related to hiring, firing, promotions, compensation, and other terms and conditions of employment based on these protected characteristics. It applies to employers with 15 or more employees, including private businesses, labor organizations, and government agencies.

3.2 Equal Pay Act:

The Equal Pay Act (EPA) aims to ensure that men and women receive equal pay for equal work. It prohibits pay discrimination based on gender, mandating that employers provide equal compensation for employees who perform substantially similar work in terms of skill, effort, responsibility, and working conditions. The EPA covers both private employers and federal, state, and local government employers.

3.3 Age Discrimination in Employment Act (ADEA):

The Age Discrimination in Employment Act (ADEA) safeguards individuals who are 40 years of age or older from discrimination in employment based on their age. It prohibits age-based discrimination in hiring, termination, promotions, compensation, and other employment-related decisions. The ADEA applies to employers with 20 or more employees and covers both private and public sector employers.

3.4 Americans with Disabilities Act (ADA):

The Americans with Disabilities Act (ADA) protects individuals with disabilities from discrimination in employment. It prohibits employers from discriminating against qualified individuals with disabilities in all aspects of employment, including hiring, firing, promotions, and reasonable accommodations. The ADA applies to employers with 15 or more employees and covers private businesses, state and local governments, and labor unions.

3.5 Pregnancy Discrimination Act (PDA):

The Pregnancy Discrimination Act (PDA) is an amendment to Title VII that prohibits employers from discriminating against employees based on pregnancy, childbirth, or related medical conditions. It mandates that employers treat pregnant employees the same as other employees with similar abilities or limitations. The PDA applies to employers with 15 or more employees.

3.6 Genetic Information Nondiscrimination Act (GINA):

The Genetic Information Nondiscrimination Act (GINA) prohibits employers from using an individual's genetic information in making employment decisions, including hiring, firing, promotions, and benefits. It protects individuals from discrimination based on their genetic information or family medical history. GINA applies to employers with 15 or more employees.

Understanding these anti-discrimination laws is essential for both employers and employees to foster a workplace environment that promotes fairness, equality, and inclusivity. Employers must establish policies and practices that comply with these laws, while employees should be aware of their rights and protections to address any instances of discrimination.

Anti-discrimination laws play a critical role in ensuring equal treatment and opportunities in the workplace. Title VII, the EPA, ADEA, ADA, PDA, and GINA provide comprehensive protection against discrimination based on various protected characteristics such as race, color, religion, sex, national origin, age, disability, pregnancy, and genetic information. By understanding and adhering to these laws, employers can create a workplace free from discrimination, fostering a diverse and inclusive environment. Likewise, employees can assert their rights and seek remedies if they experience discriminatory practices. It is essential for employers and employees to be well-informed about these anti-discrimination laws to promote a fair and equitable work culture.

Chapter 4: Wage and Hour Laws

Wage and hour laws are designed to protect employees by ensuring fair compensation for their work and regulating working hours. This chapter explores key federal laws that govern wages, minimum wage requirements, overtime pay, and exemptions. Understanding these laws is crucial for both employers and employees to ensure compliance and uphold fair labor practices.

4.1 Fair Labor Standards Act (FLSA):

The Fair Labor Standards Act (FLSA) is a federal law that establishes minimum wage, overtime pay, record-keeping, and child labor standards for most employees. The FLSA requires employers to pay covered nonexempt employees at least the federal minimum wage for all hours worked and overtime pay at a rate of one and a half times the regular rate for hours worked beyond 40 in a workweek. The FLSA applies to employers engaged in interstate commerce or that meet specific enterprise coverage thresholds.

4.2 Minimum Wage:

The FLSA sets the federal minimum wage, which is the lowest hourly rate that covered nonexempt employees must be paid. However, individual states may have their own minimum wage laws, and employers must comply with whichever requirement–federal or state– is higher. It is essential for employers to stay informed about applicable minimum wage rates and any changes or updates to ensure compliance.

4.3 Overtime Pay:

The FLSA requires employers to pay covered nonexempt employees overtime pay at a rate of one and a half times their regular rate of pay for hours worked beyond 40 in a workweek. Certain exemptions exist for specific job categories and industries. Employers must accurately track employees' working hours and calculate overtime pay accordingly. It is important to note that some states may have additional requirements regarding overtime pay.

4.4 Exemptions from FLSA:

The FLSA provides exemptions from certain wage and hour requirements for specific categories of employees. Common exemptions include executive, administrative, professional, outside sales, and certain computer-related employees who meet specific criteria. These exemptions often depend on factors such as job duties, salary level, and method of compensation. It is crucial for employers to correctly determine whether employees qualify for exemptions to ensure compliance with the FLSA.

Understanding wage and hour laws is essential for both employers and employees. Employers must establish policies and practices that adhere to minimum wage requirements, accurately calculate and provide overtime pay, and correctly classify employees under applicable exemptions. Employees need to be aware of their rights to fair compensation and understand how wage and hour laws protect them.

Wage and hour laws, particularly the Fair Labor Standards Act (FLSA), provide crucial protections for employees regarding fair compensation and working hours. By complying with these laws, employers can ensure that employees receive at least the minimum wage, appropriate overtime pay, and accurate record-keeping. Employees, on the other hand, can be aware of their rights and take necessary steps to address any wage and hour violations. Understanding these laws fosters a fair and balanced work environment while upholding employee rights. It is important for employers and employees to stay informed about wage and hour laws, including any federal or state-specific requirements or updates.

Chapter 5: Family and Medical Leave

Family and Medical Leave laws are designed to provide employees with job-protected leave for certain qualifying events, such as the birth or adoption of a child, serious health conditions, or caring for a family member with a serious health condition. This chapter explores the Family and Medical Leave Act (FMLA), which establishes the rights and obligations of employers and employees regarding leave entitlement, eligibility requirements, and employer obligations.

5.1 Family and Medical Leave Act (FMLA):

The Family and Medical Leave Act (FMLA) is a federal law that grants eligible employees the right to take up to 12 weeks of unpaid leave in a 12-month period for specified family and medical reasons. FMLA leave can be taken for the birth or adoption of a child, the care of a seriously ill family member, or the employee's own serious health condition. The FMLA applies to employers with 50 or more employees within a 75-mile radius.

5.2 Eligibility and Employee Rights:

To be eligible for FMLA leave, employees must have worked for their employer for at least 12 months and have accumulated a minimum of 1,250 hours of service during the previous 12-month period. Eligible employees have the right to take FMLA leave without fear of job loss and have their health benefits maintained during the leave period.

FMLA leave can be taken all at once or intermittently, depending on the specific circumstances. It provides job protection, meaning that upon return from FMLA leave, employees generally have the right to be restored to their original position or an equivalent position with equivalent pay, benefits, and working conditions.

5.3 Employer Obligations:

Employers covered by the FMLA have specific obligations to comply with the law. These obligations include providing employees with notice of their rights and responsibilities under the FMLA, maintaining employee health benefits during FMLA leave, and restoring employees to their original positions or equivalent positions upon their return.

Employers must also maintain accurate records of FMLA leave, including the dates and hours of leave taken by each employee, and adhere to confidentiality requirements regarding an employee's medical information.

Understanding the FMLA is crucial for both employers and employees. Employers must ensure compliance with FMLA requirements, accurately determine employee eligibility for leave, and maintain appropriate records. Employees need to be aware of their rights under the FMLA, properly notify their employers of their intention to take FMLA leave, and understand the reinstatement rights upon their return.

The Family and Medical Leave Act (FMLA) provides employees with important protections and rights regarding job-protected leave for qualifying family and medical reasons. By understanding the FMLA's provisions, both employers and employees can navigate the leave entitlement, eligibility requirements, and employer obligations associated with FMLA leave.

Compliance with the FMLA ensures that eligible employees can take leave without fear of job loss, maintain their health benefits, and have the right to return to their positions or equivalent positions upon completion of their FMLA leave. Employers must be knowledgeable about the FMLA's requirements to properly administer leave and fulfill their obligations.

Employees should understand their rights and responsibilities under the FMLA, communicate with their employers about their need for leave, and adhere to any notification or documentation requirements. By effectively navigating the FMLA, employers and employees can create a supportive work environment that recognizes and accommodates employees' family and medical needs.

Chapter 6: Workplace Safety and Health

Workplace safety and health are paramount in ensuring the well-being of employees and maintaining a productive work environment. This chapter explores the laws and regulations governing workplace safety and health in the United States, with a focus on the Occupational Safety and Health Act (OSHA). Understanding these laws is crucial for both employers and employees to create a safe and healthy work environment.

6.1 Occupational Safety and Health Act (OSHA):

The Occupational Safety and Health Act (OSHA) is a federal law that aims to ensure safe and healthful working conditions for employees. OSHA sets forth standards and regulations that employers must follow to protect employees from workplace hazards. It covers most private sector employers and their employees, as well as some public sector employers.

OSHA requires employers to provide a workplace free from recognized hazards that may cause serious harm or death. Employers must comply with specific safety and health standards relevant to their industries, conduct hazard assessments, implement safety programs, and provide training and education to employees.

6.2 Employer Responsibilities:

Employers have several key responsibilities under OSHA to ensure workplace safety and health. These responsibilities include:

a) Providing a Safe and Healthy Work Environment: Employers must identify and address workplace hazards, implement necessary safety measures, and promote a culture of safety among employees.

b) Compliance with OSHA Standards: Employers must adhere to specific OSHA standards and regulations applicable to their industry. These standards cover a wide range of areas, including hazardous materials, machinery safety, electrical safety, respiratory protection, and more.

c) Hazard Assessments: Employers must regularly assess workplace hazards, conduct inspections, and identify potential risks to employee safety and health. This includes investigating accidents or near-miss incidents and taking corrective actions to prevent future occurrences.

d) Training and Education: Employers must provide comprehensive training and education programs to employees regarding workplace safety, hazards, emergency procedures, and the proper use of personal protective equipment (PPE).

6.3 Employee Rights:

Employees also have rights and responsibilities related to workplace safety and health. These include:

a) Right to a Safe and Healthy Work Environment: Employees have the right to work in an environment free from hazards that may cause harm or injury. They should report unsafe conditions to their employers and actively participate in safety programs.

b) Access to Information: Employees have the right to access information regarding workplace hazards, safety standards, and their rights under OSHA. Employers must provide employees with information related to hazardous materials, safety data sheets (SDS), and safety training materials.

c) Whistleblower Protection: Employees have protection against retaliation for reporting workplace safety concerns or filing complaints with OSHA. Employers cannot take adverse actions, such as termination or demotion, against employees who exercise their rights under OSHA.

6.4 Safety Standards and Inspections:

OSHA conducts workplace inspections to ensure employers' compliance with safety standards. Inspections may be scheduled or unannounced, depending on the circumstances. Employers are required to cooperate with OSHA inspectors, provide access to workplace records and facilities, and address any identified violations promptly.

Examples of safety standards enforced by OSHA include machine guarding requirements, chemical hazard communication, fall protection measures, electrical safety standards, and personal protective equipment (PPE) requirements.

Workplace safety and health are of utmost importance in any organization. By understanding and complying with the Occupational Safety and Health Act (OSHA) and its regulations, employers can create a safe and healthy work environment, protect their employees from hazards, and mitigate the risk of accidents and injuries.

Employees should be aware of their rights, actively participate in safety programs, and report any unsafe conditions to their employers. By fostering a culture of safety and implementing necessary measures, employers and employees can work together to promote a workplace environment that prioritizes the well-being of all individuals.

Chapter 7: Employee Benefits

Employee benefits play a vital role in attracting and retaining a talented workforce. This chapter explores key federal laws and regulations that govern employee benefits in the United States. Understanding these laws is essential for both employers and employees to navigate the complexities of employee benefit programs and ensure compliance with legal requirements.

7.1 Employee Retirement Income Security Act (ERISA):

The Employee Retirement Income Security Act (ERISA) is a federal law that sets standards for private sector employee benefit plans. ERISA applies to employer-sponsored retirement plans, such as pension plans and 401(k) plans, as well as health and welfare benefit plans, including group health insurance, disability insurance, and life insurance plans.

ERISA establishes rules for plan administration, reporting and disclosure, fiduciary responsibilities, and participants' rights. It requires employers to provide participants with information about their benefits, including plan features, funding, vesting, and procedures for filing claims and appeals.

7.2 Health Insurance Portability and Accountability Act (HIPAA):

The Health Insurance Portability and Accountability Act (HIPAA) protects individuals' rights to maintain health insurance coverage when changing or losing jobs. HIPAA ensures the portability and availability of health coverage, limits pre-existing condition exclusions, and prohibits discrimination based on health status.

HIPAA also establishes privacy and security standards for protected health information (PHI). Employers must safeguard the privacy of employees' health information and implement measures to secure electronic PHI.

7.3 Affordable Care Act (ACA):

The Affordable Care Act (ACA) has significantly impacted the landscape of employee health benefits. It requires certain employers to offer affordable health insurance coverage to their full-time employees or face penalties. The ACA also mandates essential health benefits that must be included in health insurance plans, such as preventive care, maternity care, mental health services, and prescription drug coverage.

Additionally, the ACA introduced health insurance marketplaces where individuals can shop for coverage, often with the assistance of premium subsidies or tax credits based on income eligibility.

7.4 Employee Assistance Programs (EAPs):

Employee Assistance Programs (EAPs) are employer-sponsored programs designed to assist employees with personal or work-related challenges. EAPs often provide counseling services, referral resources, and support for various issues, including mental health, substance abuse, stress management, and work-life balance.

While there is no federal law specifically governing EAPs, they may be subject to certain privacy requirements under HIPAA if they provide services that involve protected health information.

Understanding these employee benefit laws is crucial for employers to establish compliant benefit programs and for employees to navigate their rights and entitlements.

Employee benefits are a critical component of the employer-employee relationship. By understanding and complying with laws such as ERISA, HIPAA, and the ACA, employers can design and administer employee benefit programs that provide valuable coverage and protect employees' rights. Employees should be familiar with their rights under these laws, including the right to access and understand their benefits, the portability of health coverage, and the availability of assistance programs. By effectively managing employee benefits, employers and employees can create a positive work environment that supports the well-being and financial security of the workforce.

Part II: Government Agencies and Enforcement

Chapter 8: Equal Employment Opportunity Commission (EEOC)

The Equal Employment Opportunity Commission (EEOC) is a key government agency responsible for enforcing federal laws that prohibit workplace discrimination. This chapter explores the role and functions of the EEOC, its complaint process, and the protections it provides to employees. Understanding the EEOC's role is essential for both employers and employees to ensure compliance with anti-discrimination laws and address any instances of discrimination effectively.

8.1 Role and Functions:

The EEOC plays a crucial role in promoting equal employment opportunities and combating workplace discrimination. Its primary functions include:

a) Enforcement: The EEOC investigates complaints of employment discrimination filed by individuals against employers. It has the authority to initiate investigations and take legal action against employers found to have violated federal anti-discrimination laws.

b) Education and Outreach: The EEOC conducts educational programs and outreach initiatives to raise awareness about workplace discrimination, employee rights, and employer responsibilities. These programs aim to inform the public, employers, and employees about their rights and obligations under federal anti-discrimination laws.

c) Guidance and Technical Assistance: The EEOC provides guidance and technical assistance to employers and employees regarding compliance with federal anti-discrimination laws. This assistance includes issuing regulations, interpretive guidance, and advisory opinions to help employers and employees understand their rights and obligations.

d) Mediation and Conciliation: The EEOC offers mediation and conciliation services as an alternative to litigation. Through these processes, the EEOC facilitates negotiations between employers and employees to reach a resolution and avoid costly legal proceedings.

8.2 Filing a Complaint:

Employees who believe they have been subjected to workplace discrimination can file a complaint with the EEOC. The complaint process typically involves the following steps:

a) Filing a Charge: The employee files a charge of discrimination with the EEOC within a specified time period, usually 180 days or 300 days from the alleged discriminatory act, depending on the jurisdiction. The charge outlines the details of the alleged discrimination, including the parties involved, the nature of the discrimination, and the harm suffered.

b) EEOC Investigation: Upon receiving a charge, the EEOC initiates an investigation to determine the merits of the complaint. This may involve interviews, requests for documentation, and fact-finding efforts to gather evidence related to the alleged discrimination.

c) Mediation or Litigation: Depending on the circumstances and the outcome of the investigation, the EEOC may offer mediation services to facilitate a resolution between the parties. If mediation is unsuccessful or not pursued, the EEOC may choose to litigate the case on behalf of the aggrieved employee or issue a right-to-sue letter, allowing the employee to file a lawsuit in court.

8.3 Protections and Remedies:

The EEOC provides several protections and remedies to individuals who experience workplace discrimination. These include:

a) Protection against Retaliation: The EEOC enforces provisions that prohibit employers from retaliating against employees who assert their rights under anti-discrimination laws. Employees who engage in protected activities, such as filing a complaint or participating in an EEOC investigation, are protected from adverse employment actions.

b) Remedies and Relief: If the EEOC finds that discrimination has occurred, it may seek remedies on behalf of the aggrieved employee. These remedies may include back pay, reinstatement, promotion, compensatory damages, and injunctive relief to prevent further discrimination.

c) Systemic Investigations and Lawsuits: The EEOC also conducts systemic investigations to address patterns or practices of discrimination that affect a group of individuals or an entire workplace. If systemic discrimination is found, the EEOC may file a lawsuit against the employer to seek broader remedies and effect systemic change.

Understanding the role of the EEOC and its complaint process empowers both employers and employees to navigate workplace discrimination issues effectively and ensure compliance with anti-discrimination laws.

The Equal Employment Opportunity Commission (EEOC) plays a pivotal role in enforcing federal anti-discrimination laws and promoting equal employment opportunities. Employers and employees should be familiar with the EEOC's functions, the complaint process, and the protections it provides to individuals who experience workplace discrimination.

By understanding the role of the EEOC, employers can take proactive steps to prevent discrimination, create inclusive work environments, and address complaints effectively. Employees, on the other hand, can assert their rights, file complaints, and seek redress for discriminatory actions. Ultimately, the EEOC serves as a vital resource in ensuring workplace equality and combating discrimination in the United States.

Chapter 9: Department of Labor (DOL)

The Department of Labor (DOL) is a federal agency responsible for promoting and protecting the welfare of workers in the United States. This chapter explores the role and functions of the DOL, focusing on its key divisions: the Wage and Hour Division (WHD), the Occupational Safety and Health Administration (OSHA), and the Office of Federal Contract Compliance Programs (OFCCP). Understanding the DOL's responsibilities is crucial for both employers and employees to ensure compliance with labor laws and promote fair and safe working conditions.

9.1 Wage and Hour Division (WHD):

The Wage and Hour Division (WHD) of the DOL enforces various federal labor laws related to wages, hours, and employment conditions. The WHD's key responsibilities include:

a) Minimum Wage and Overtime: The WHD enforces the federal minimum wage, which establishes the lowest hourly rate employers must pay covered nonexempt employees. It also ensures that covered employees receive overtime pay at a rate of one and a half times their regular rate for hours worked beyond 40 in a workweek.

b) Family and Medical Leave Act (FMLA): The WHD administers and enforces the FMLA, which provides eligible employees with job-protected leave for specific family and medical reasons. The WHD ensures compliance with FMLA requirements, investigates complaints, and provides guidance to employers and employees.

c) Record-Keeping and Compliance: The WHD monitors employers' compliance with record-keeping requirements, which include maintaining accurate records of employees' wages, hours worked, and other employment-related information. It conducts investigations and audits to ensure compliance with wage and hour laws.

9.2 Occupational Safety and Health Administration (OSHA):

The Occupational Safety and Health Administration (OSHA) is a division of the DOL dedicated to ensuring safe and healthy working conditions for employees. OSHA's key responsibilities include:

a) Workplace Safety Regulations: OSHA sets and enforces safety and health standards to protect employees from workplace hazards. It establishes regulations related to hazard communication, machinery safety, personal protective equipment (PPE), electrical safety, and more.

b) Inspections and Compliance: OSHA conducts inspections of workplaces to ensure compliance with safety regulations. Inspections may be scheduled or unannounced, and employers are required to cooperate with OSHA inspectors, provide access to facilities and records, and address identified violations promptly.

c) Training and Education: OSHA provides training and education programs to employers and employees to promote safety and raise awareness about workplace hazards. It offers resources, guidelines, and assistance to help employers create and maintain safe working environments.

9.3 Office of Federal Contract Compliance Programs (OFCCP):

The Office of Federal Contract Compliance Programs (OFCCP) is responsible for ensuring that federal contractors and subcontractors comply with equal employment opportunity and affirmative action requirements. The OFCCP's main functions include:

a) Affirmative Action Compliance: The OFCCP enforces affirmative action requirements for federal contractors, which aim to promote equal employment opportunities and eliminate discrimination in hiring, promotions, and other employment practices.

b) Compliance Evaluations: The OFCCP conducts compliance evaluations of federal contractors to assess their adherence to equal employment opportunity requirements. These evaluations may involve audits, data analysis, and on-site visits to ensure compliance with federal regulations.

c) Technical Assistance: The OFCCP provides technical assistance and guidance to federal contractors to help them understand and comply with their affirmative action obligations. It offers resources, training, and support to promote diversity and inclusion in the workplace.

Understanding the role of the Department of Labor (DOL) and its divisions is essential for employers to ensure compliance with labor laws and create safe and fair working conditions. Employees benefit from knowing their rights and the protections provided by the DOL. By working in collaboration with the DOL, employers and employees can contribute to a more equitable and secure labor landscape.

The Department of Labor (DOL) plays a crucial role in safeguarding the rights and welfare of workers in the United States. The Wage and Hour Division (WHD), Occupational Safety and Health Administration (OSHA), and Office of Federal Contract Compliance Programs (OFCCP) are key divisions within the DOL, each with specific responsibilities related to labor standards, workplace safety, and equal employment opportunities.

Employers should familiarize themselves with the regulations enforced by these divisions to ensure compliance and promote fair and safe working conditions. Employees, on the other hand, can benefit from understanding their rights and protections provided by the DOL. By working in partnership with the DOL, employers and employees contribute to a harmonious and equitable work environment that prioritizes the well-being and rights of workers.

Chapter 10: National Labor Relations Board (NLRB)

The National Labor Relations Board (NLRB) is a federal agency responsible for enforcing and protecting the rights of employees and employers in relation to collective bargaining and labor relations in the United States. This chapter explores the role and functions of the NLRB, including employee rights to organize, unfair labor practices, and the process of collective bargaining. Understanding the NLRB's role is essential for both employers and employees to navigate labor relations effectively and ensure compliance with federal labor laws.

10.1 Employee Rights to Organize:

The NLRB safeguards employees' rights to engage in concerted activities, including the right to form, join, or assist labor organizations. Key aspects of employee rights to organize include:

a) Unionization: Employees have the right to form, join, or assist labor unions for the purpose of collective bargaining. The NLRB protects employees from interference, restraint, or coercion by employers in exercising their rights to unionize.

b) Representation Elections: When a group of employees seeks representation by a union, the NLRB oversees the process of conducting representation elections. These elections allow employees to decide whether they want a specific union to represent them in collective bargaining with the employer.

c) Bargaining Unit Determination: The NLRB determines the appropriate bargaining unit, which defines the group of employees who will be represented by the union for collective bargaining purposes.

10.2 Unfair Labor Practices:

The NLRB enforces regulations regarding unfair labor practices committed by employers or labor organizations that interfere with employees' rights. Common unfair labor practices include:

a) Interference or Coercion: Employers are prohibited from interfering with, restraining, or coercing employees in the exercise of their rights to engage in collective bargaining, form or join labor organizations, or engage in other concerted activities protected by the National Labor Relations Act (NLRA).

b) Discrimination: Employers cannot discriminate against employees for engaging in protected activities, such as supporting or participating in union activities or filing unfair labor practice charges.

c) Failure to Bargain in Good Faith: Both employers and labor organizations are required to bargain in good faith regarding terms and conditions of employment. Failing to engage in meaningful negotiations or refusing to reach an agreement may constitute an unfair labor practice.

10.3 Collective Bargaining:

Collective bargaining is the process through which employers and labor organizations negotiate terms and conditions of employment, such as wages, benefits, and working conditions, on behalf of employees. The NLRB plays a crucial role in overseeing and facilitating the collective bargaining process, which includes:

a) Duty to Bargain: Employers have a legal obligation to bargain in good faith with the labor organization representing their employees. This includes exchanging proposals, providing relevant information, and engaging in meaningful negotiations.

b) Impasse and Dispute Resolution: If parties reach an impasse in negotiations, the NLRB may provide assistance in resolving disputes, including mediation or arbitration, to facilitate the collective bargaining process.

c) Collective Bargaining Agreements: Once an agreement is reached, it is formalized in a collective bargaining agreement (CBA), which outlines the terms and conditions of employment for the represented employees.

Understanding the role of the National Labor Relations Board (NLRB) is crucial for employers, employees, and labor organizations to navigate labor relations effectively and ensure compliance with federal labor laws.

The National Labor Relations Board (NLRB) plays a critical role in protecting the rights of employees and employers in relation to labor relations and collective bargaining. By understanding the NLRB's role and functions, employers can ensure compliance with labor laws, engage in good-faith bargaining, and respect employees' rights to organize. Employees and labor organizations benefit from knowing their rights and protections under the NLRA and working with the NLRB to pursue fair and equitable labor practices.

Through its oversight and enforcement, the NLRB contributes to fostering a balanced and constructive labor environment where employees can exercise their rights to organize and engage in collective bargaining, and employers can negotiate in good faith. By upholding the principles of the NLRA, the NLRB promotes effective labor relations that benefit both workers and employers in the United States.

Part III: Special Employment Issues

Chapter 11: Immigration Law and Employment

Immigration law and employment intersect in various ways, as employers often hire foreign workers to meet their labor needs. This chapter explores key aspects of immigration law that impact employment in the United States. Understanding these laws is crucial for employers to navigate the process of hiring foreign workers and ensuring compliance with immigration regulations.

11.1 Immigration Reform and Control Act (IRCA):

The Immigration Reform and Control Act (IRCA) is a federal law that establishes requirements for employers when hiring employees and aims to prevent unauthorized employment of individuals who are not legally authorized to work in the United States. Key aspects of IRCA include:

a) Employment Verification: IRCA mandates that employers verify the identity and employment eligibility of their employees by completing Form I-9, which requires employees to present specific documents that establish their identity and authorization to work.

b) Prohibition of Discrimination: IRCA prohibits employers from discriminating against employees on the basis of their national origin or citizenship status. Employers must treat all individuals equally during the hiring process and employment.

11.2 Employer Compliance and Verification:

Employers are responsible for complying with immigration laws and ensuring the employment eligibility of their workforce. To achieve compliance, employers must:

a) Form I-9 Completion: Employers must properly complete and retain Form I-9 for each employee, verifying their identity and employment eligibility. This includes reviewing acceptable documents provided by the employee and ensuring the form is completed accurately and timely.

b) E-Verify: While not mandatory for all employers, E-Verify is an electronic system that allows employers to verify the employment eligibility of newly hired employees. Participating employers enter the information from an employee's Form I-9 into the E-Verify system to confirm their work authorization.

c) Anti-Discrimination Policies: Employers should establish and enforce anti-discrimination policies to ensure fair treatment of all employees, regardless of their national origin or citizenship status. Discrimination based on immigration status is prohibited under IRCA.

11.3 Work Visas and Employment-Based Immigration:

Employers may seek to hire foreign workers through work visas and employment-based immigration programs. Common work visas include:

a) H-1B Visa: This visa is for foreign workers in specialty occupations that require specialized knowledge. Employers must demonstrate that there are no qualified U.S. workers available for the position.

b) L-1 Visa: This visa is for intracompany transferees who are transferred to a U.S. branch, parent, affiliate, or subsidiary of their current employer.

c) O Visa: This visa is for individuals with extraordinary ability in fields such as science, education, business, athletics, or the arts.

d) PERM Labor Certification: Some employment-based immigration processes require employers to obtain a labor certification from the Department of Labor, demonstrating that there are no qualified U.S. workers available for the position.

11.4 Compliance with Immigration Laws:

To ensure compliance with immigration laws, employers should:

a) Stay Informed: Employers should stay updated on changes and updates to immigration laws and regulations to ensure compliance in the hiring and employment of foreign workers.

b) Document Retention: Employers must maintain accurate and complete records related to the hiring and employment of foreign workers, including Form I-9s, visa petitions, labor certifications, and supporting documentation.

c) Immigration Audits: Employers may be subject to immigration audits and investigations to ensure compliance with immigration laws. It is crucial to cooperate with government agencies during these audits and address any identified issues promptly.

Understanding the intricacies of immigration law as it relates to employment is essential for employers to navigate the process of hiring foreign workers legally and complying with immigration regulations. By adhering to immigration laws, employers can create a diverse and inclusive workforce while fulfilling their legal obligations.

Immigration law and employment regulations intersect when employers hire foreign workers to meet their labor needs. By understanding the key provisions of immigration law, such as the Immigration Reform and Control Act (IRCA) and the requirements for employment verification, employers can navigate the process of hiring and employing foreign workers in compliance with immigration regulations.

Employer compliance and verification, including completing Form I-9, utilizing the E-Verify system, and implementing anti-discrimination policies, are crucial steps for employers to ensure compliance with immigration laws and provide equal opportunities for all employees. Understanding the various work visas and employment-based immigration programs allows employers to leverage these options when seeking foreign talent for specific roles.

By following the guidelines outlined in this chapter, employers can successfully navigate immigration law and employment regulations, foster a diverse workforce, and contribute to a thriving and inclusive work environment.

Chapter 12: Privacy and Data Protection

Privacy and data protection are critical considerations in today's digital age, particularly in the workplace. This chapter explores the importance of privacy and data protection in the employment context, highlighting key laws and regulations that safeguard employee privacy rights. Understanding these laws is essential for both employers and employees to strike the right balance between utilizing technology and protecting individual privacy.

12.1 Employee Privacy Rights:

Employees have a legitimate expectation of privacy in the workplace, even though employers have a vested interest in monitoring and ensuring productivity. Key aspects of employee privacy rights include:

a) Personal Information: Employees have the right to expect that their personal information, such as Social Security numbers, financial details, and medical records, will be handled confidentially and protected from unauthorized access.

b) Electronic Communications: Employees may have expectations of privacy regarding their electronic communications, such as emails, instant messages, and other electronic data. Employers should have clear policies on electronic communication monitoring to strike a balance between business needs and employee privacy.

c) Monitoring and Surveillance: While employers have the right to monitor and surveil employees in certain circumstances, such as to maintain security or prevent misconduct, it must be done in compliance with applicable laws and regulations.

12.2 Electronic Communications Privacy Act (ECPA):

The Electronic Communications Privacy Act (ECPA) is a federal law that protects electronic communications and governs their interception and disclosure. Key aspects of the ECPA include:

a) Wiretap Act: The ECPA prohibits the interception of wire, oral, or electronic communications, with limited exceptions. Employers must obtain appropriate consent or meet specific statutory requirements before monitoring or intercepting electronic communications.

b) Stored Communications Act: The ECPA also restricts the disclosure of stored electronic communications held by third-party service providers. Employers must be mindful of their obligations when accessing or disclosing employees' electronic communications stored on company servers or cloud platforms.

12.3 Data Breach Notification Laws:

Data breach notification laws require employers to notify affected individuals and appropriate authorities if a breach of personal information occurs. These laws vary by jurisdiction, but typically mandate timely notification to individuals whose personal data has been compromised.

Employers must take steps to safeguard personal information, implement security measures, and develop incident response plans to effectively address data breaches and mitigate harm.

12.4 Balancing Employer Interests and Employee Privacy:

Employers must strike a delicate balance between their legitimate business interests and employees' privacy rights. They should consider implementing the following practices:

a) Privacy Policies and Notices: Employers should develop clear and comprehensive privacy policies that outline their practices regarding the collection, use, and protection of employee personal information. Employees should be informed of their rights and expectations of privacy.

b) Consent and Authorization: Employers should obtain appropriate consent or authorization from employees before collecting, using, or disclosing their personal information. Consent should be voluntary, informed, and specific to the intended purposes.

c) Data Security Measures: Employers should implement reasonable security measures to protect employee personal information from unauthorized access, use, or disclosure. This may include encryption, access controls, firewalls, and regular security audits.

d) Employee Training and Awareness: Employers should provide training and awareness programs to employees about privacy policies, data protection practices, and the importance of maintaining confidentiality.

Privacy and data protection are vital considerations in the modern workplace. Employers must respect and protect employee privacy rights while fulfilling their legitimate business interests. By adhering to laws such as the Electronic Communications Privacy Act (ECPA), implementing comprehensive privacy policies, and safeguarding personal information, employers can create a workplace that respects employee privacy and maintains data security.

Employees, on the other hand, should be aware of their privacy rights, understand the limitations on privacy expectations in the workplace, and actively engage with employer policies and practices to protect their personal information.

By striking the right balance between employer interests and employee privacy, organizations can cultivate a culture of trust, respect, and transparency, fostering a positive work environment while ensuring the protection of sensitive employee data.

Chapter 13: Employment Termination and Severance

Employment termination is an inevitable part of the employment relationship. This chapter explores the key considerations surrounding employment termination and severance in the United States. Understanding the legal and practical aspects of termination and severance is crucial for both employers and employees to navigate this process with fairness, compliance, and professionalism.

13.1 Wrongful Termination:

Wrongful termination refers to the unlawful termination of an employee that violates federal or state laws or breaches an employment contract. Common grounds for wrongful termination include:

a) Discrimination: Termination based on an employee's protected characteristics, such as race, gender, age, religion, national origin, or disability, may constitute wrongful termination under anti-discrimination laws.

b) Retaliation: Terminating an employee in retaliation for exercising their legal rights, such as reporting workplace misconduct or participating in a complaint or investigation, is prohibited by law.

c) Breach of Contract: If an employment contract includes specific terms and conditions for termination, disregarding those terms without legal justification may be considered wrongful termination.

13.2 Layoffs and Reductions in Force:

Layoffs and reductions in force occur when employers need to downsize their workforce due to economic or operational reasons. Key considerations in these situations include:

a) WARN Act Compliance: The Worker Adjustment and Retraining Notification (WARN) Act requires employers with a certain number of employees to provide advance notice of impending mass layoffs or plant closings.

b) Severance Packages: Employers may offer severance packages to employees affected by layoffs or reductions in force as a gesture of goodwill. These packages typically include financial compensation, continuation of benefits, job placement assistance, and other provisions.

13.3 Severance Agreements:

Severance agreements are legally binding contracts between employers and employees that outline the terms and conditions of separation. Key elements of severance agreements include:

a) Consideration: In exchange for the employee's agreement to release legal claims against the employer, the employer provides certain benefits, such as additional compensation, extended benefits, or non-monetary considerations.

b) Non-Disclosure and Non-Compete Clauses: Severance agreements may include provisions that restrict the employee from disclosing confidential information or competing with the employer for a specified period.

c) Consultation with Legal Counsel: It is advisable for employees to consult with legal counsel before signing a severance agreement to ensure they understand the terms and implications.

d) Age Discrimination Considerations: The Older Workers Benefit Protection Act (OWBPA) imposes specific requirements when offering severance agreements to employees over 40 years of age, including a 21-day review period and a 7-day revocation period.

Employment termination and severance require careful attention to legal requirements, fairness, and clear communication. Employers should ensure compliance with applicable laws, provide proper notice, and consider offering reasonable severance packages. Employees, on the other hand, should understand their rights, seek legal advice when needed, and carefully review and negotiate severance agreements to protect their interests.

Employment termination and severance are significant aspects of the employment relationship. By understanding the legal obligations and best practices surrounding termination, employers can handle these situations professionally and with fairness. Employees should be aware of their rights, understand the reasons for termination, and navigate the severance process thoughtfully.

Open communication, adherence to laws and contracts, and consideration of the impact on employees' livelihoods are crucial in conducting employment terminations and offering severance packages. By approaching these matters with integrity and compassion, employers can uphold their reputation while employees can secure a smoother transition during this challenging period.

Conclusions

Employment Law and Regulations: A Comprehensive Guide provides a detailed exploration of the various legal aspects governing employers and employees. Throughout the chapters, we have delved into employment law basics, anti-discrimination laws, wage and hour laws, workplace safety and health, employee benefits, government agencies and enforcement, special employment issues, privacy and data protection, and employment termination and severance.

This comprehensive guide serves as a valuable resource for both employers and employees, offering a deep understanding of their rights, obligations, and protections within the realm of employment law. By familiarizing themselves with these laws and regulations, employers can create fair and compliant workplaces that prioritize the well-being and rights of their employees. Employees, on the other hand, can assert their rights, recognize potential violations, and seek appropriate remedies when necessary.

However, it is important to note that employment law is a complex and evolving field. Laws and regulations may change over time, and specific circumstances can significantly impact legal outcomes. Therefore, it is advisable to consult legal professionals and up-to-date sources for comprehensive and accurate information regarding employee laws and regulations in the United States.

By fostering a deep understanding of employment law, employers can build a culture of fairness, inclusivity, and compliance. Employees can confidently navigate their rights, seek appropriate resolutions for workplace issues, and contribute to a healthy and productive work environment.

As we conclude this comprehensive guide, it is essential to recognize that the successful application of employment law requires a commitment from both employers and employees to uphold the principles of fairness, equality, and respect in the workplace. By working together and staying informed about legal rights and obligations, employers and employees can contribute to an environment that values and protects the rights of all individuals involved in the employment relationship.

Remember, employment law serves as a foundation for creating equitable workplaces where individuals can thrive and organizations can prosper. By adhering to these principles, we can collectively promote a harmonious and just employment landscape in the United States.

Glossary

At-Will Employment: A type of employment relationship in which either the employer or the employee can terminate the employment at any time and for any reason, as long as it is not in violation of any applicable laws or employment contracts.

Bargaining Unit: A group of employees represented by a labor union for the purposes of collective bargaining.

Collective Bargaining: The process in which employers and labor organizations negotiate terms and conditions of employment on behalf of employees.

Discrimination: The unfair or unequal treatment of individuals based on their protected characteristics, such as race, gender, age, religion, national origin, or disability.

E-Verify: An electronic system that allows employers to verify the employment eligibility of newly hired employees.

FMLA (Family and Medical Leave Act): A federal law that provides eligible employees with job-protected leave for specific family and medical reasons, such as the birth of a child or caring for a family member with a serious health condition.

IRCA (Immigration Reform and Control Act): A federal law that establishes requirements for employers when hiring employees and aims to prevent unauthorized employment of individuals who are not legally authorized to work in the United States.

Layoff: The temporary or permanent termination of employees from their jobs due to reasons such as economic downturn, reorganization, or business closure.

Minimum Wage: The lowest hourly wage rate that employers must legally pay their employees.

NLRB (National Labor Relations Board): A federal agency responsible for enforcing and protecting the rights of employees and employers in relation to collective bargaining and labor relations.

Severance Agreement: A legally binding contract between an employer and an employee that outlines the terms and conditions of separation, typically including compensation and benefits provided to the employee upon termination.

Termination: The act of ending an employment relationship, either by the employer (dismissal) or the employee (resignation).

WARN Act (Worker Adjustment and Retraining Notification Act): A federal law that requires employers to provide advance notice of impending mass layoffs or plant closings.

WHD (Wage and Hour Division): A division of the Department of Labor responsible for enforcing federal labor laws related to wages, hours, and employment conditions.

Work Visa: A permit granted by the government that allows foreign individuals to work in the United States for a specific period and under certain conditions.

Index

References

American Bar Association (ABA). (n.d.). *Legal resources and publications. Retrieved from* https://www.americanbar.org

Cornell Law School Legal Information Institute (LII). (n.d.). *Federal laws and regulations. Retrieved from* https://www.law.cornell.edu

Equal Employment Opportunity Commission (EEOC). (n.d.). *Anti-discrimination laws and regulations. Retrieved from* https://www.eeoc.gov

Immigration and Customs Enforcement (ICE). (n.d.). *Immigration laws and employer compliance. Retrieved from* https://www.ice.gov

Legal Information Institute (LII) at Cornell University Law School. (n.d.). *Employment statutes, case law, and regulations. Retrieved from* https://www.law.cornell.edu

National Labor Relations Board (NLRB). (n.d.). *Labor relations, collective bargaining, and unfair labor practices. Retrieved from* https://www.nlrb.gov

Occupational Safety and Health Administration (OSHA). (n.d.). *Workplace safety and health regulations. Retrieved from* https://www.osha.gov

Society for Human Resource Management (SHRM). (n.d.). *HR and employment law resources. Retrieved from* https://www.shrm.org

U.S. Citizenship and Immigration Services (USCIS). (n.d.). *Employment-based immigration information. Retrieved from* https://www.uscis.gov

U.S. Department of Labor (DOL). (n.d.). *Employment laws, regulations, and enforcement agencies. Retrieved from* https://www.dol.gov

U.S. Equal Employment Opportunity Commission (EEOC). (n.d.). *Federal anti-discrimination laws and guidelines. Retrieved from* https://www.eeoc.gov

U.S. Department of Labor (DOL). (n.d.). *Employment laws, wage and hour regulations, and workplace safety standards. Retrieved from* https://www.dol.gov

About the Author

Dr. Raul Dominguez is a Ph.D. in Industrial-Organizational (IO) Psychology, specializing in employment law. Their expertise combines IO psychology and employment law, providing unique insights into employee selection, performance management, and workplace behavior. Dr. Dominguez's book offers practical guidance, equipping employers and HR professionals to create legally compliant, inclusive, high-performing work environments. Their work promotes fairness, diversity, and employee well-being, enhancing organizational cultures and productivity.

Cover artwork and Story: Don Ford
Publisher's Note:

This is a work of fiction. The names,
characters, places, and events, are
the work of the author's imagination;
in other words they are not real. :-}

Fine Design Publishing, Don Ford
©2013

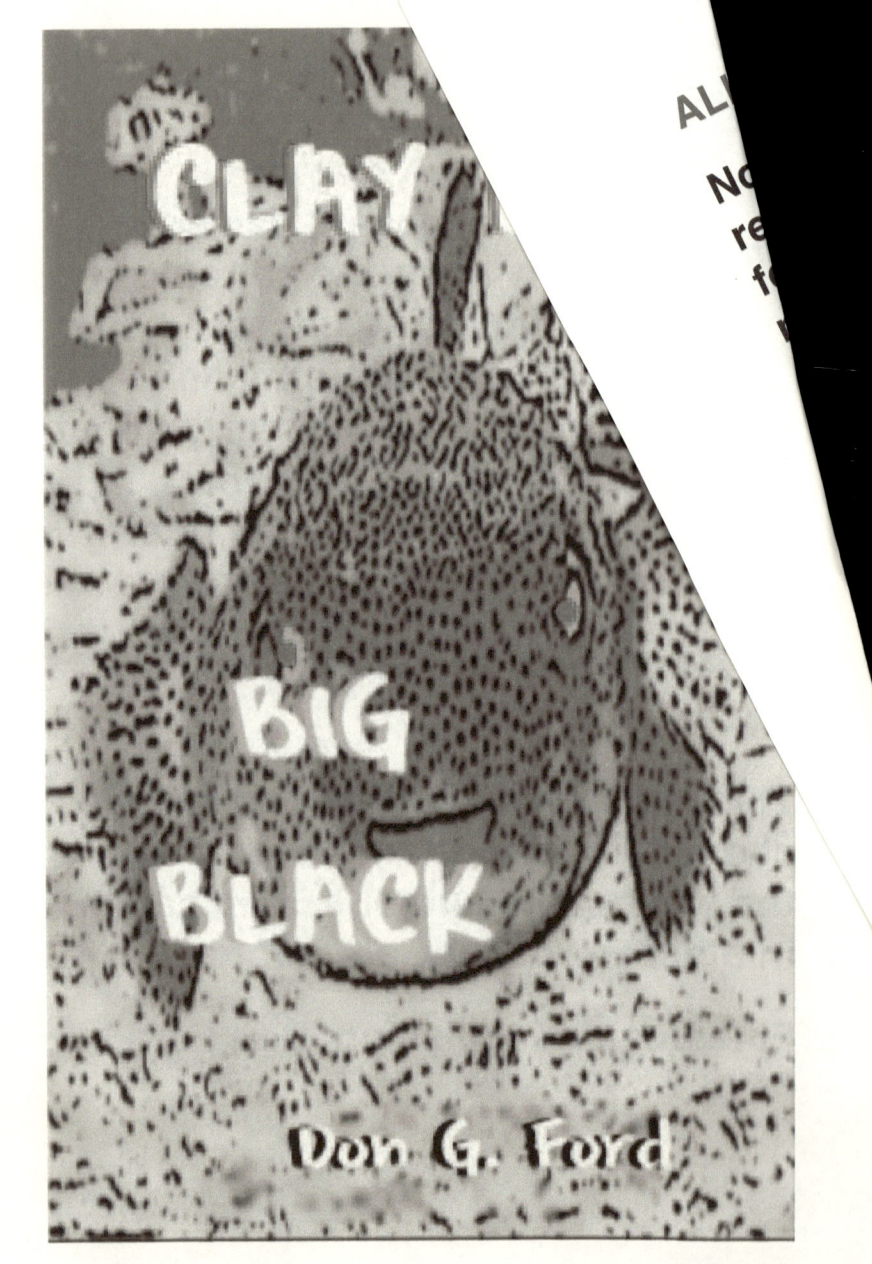

CLAY

BIG

BLACK

Don G. Ford

www.ingramcontent.com/pod-product-compliance
Lightning Source LLC
Chambersburg PA
CBHW030524290526
45786CB00004B/1605

Dedication:

This Book is dedicated to readers who enjoy good storytelling in fiction. The kids will certainly smile when reading it, or having it read to them.

The Adventure into Nature Begins Here at Clay Pond.

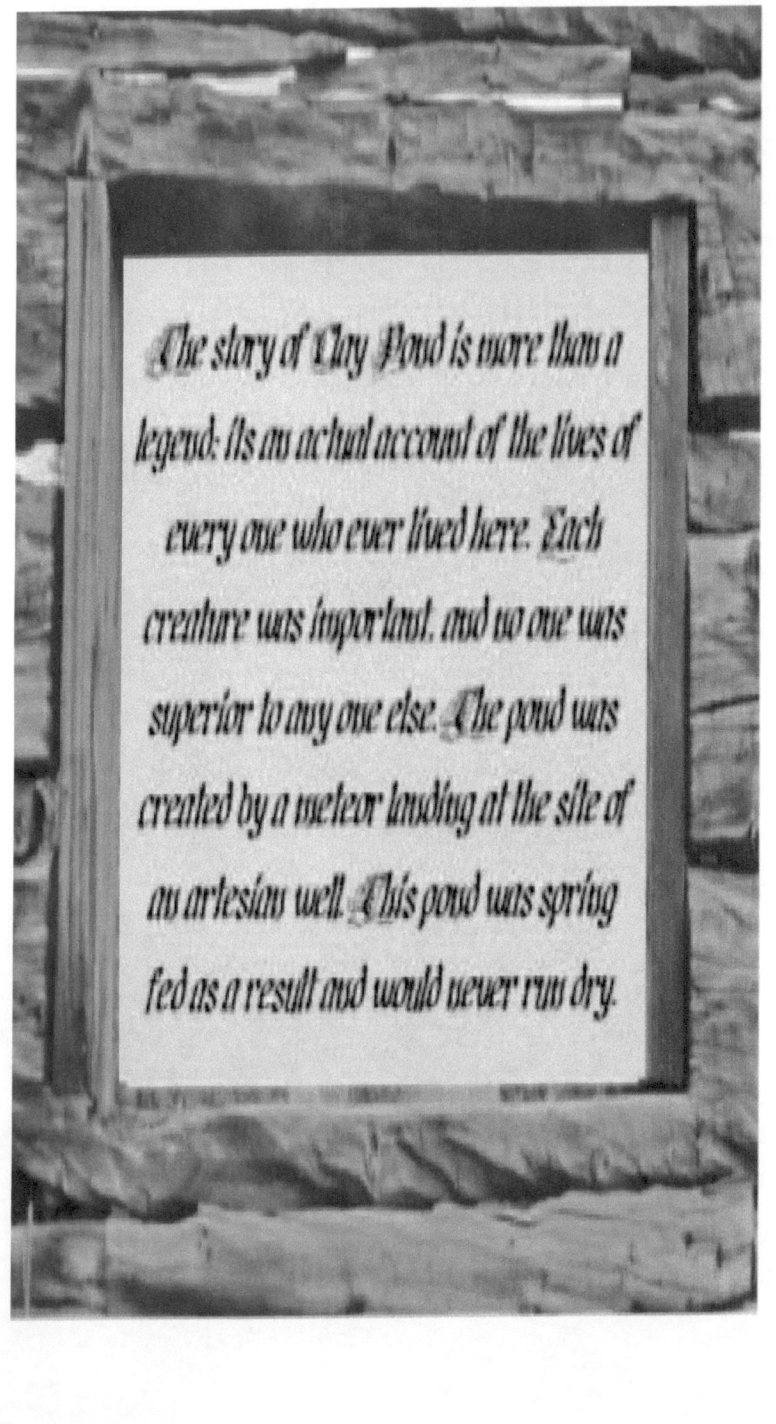

The story of Clay Pond is more than a legend: its an actual account of the lives of every one who ever lived here. Each creature was important, and no one was superior to any one else. The pond was created by a meteor landing at the site of an artesian well. This pond was spring fed as a result and would never run dry.

d.g.ford

Irises & Lilies began popping up all around the edges; touching the water. Many colors were visible, especially from the trees.

Today we meet Big Black.

Clay Pond is home to many friends. A few are enemies too. The longer you live here, the more you learn 'who is who' around the pond. Big Black is the large resident bass who hangs in the area of thick weeds near the North edge of Clay Pond.

As long as no creature on the pond goes near his living space, all is well. Big Black found it much cooler lurking among the duckweeds, where the springs of water rush into the pond. It is where more oxygen is supplied to the water, which a fish needs a fresh gulp of from time to time.

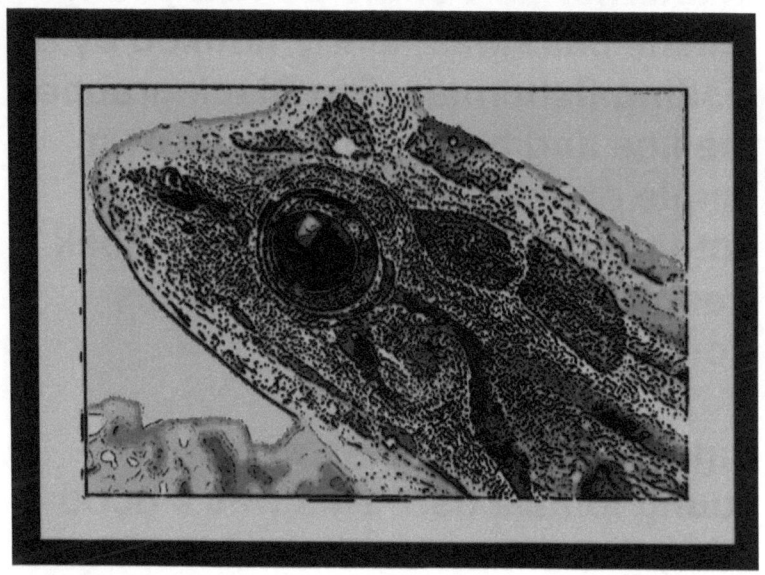

Freddie the Frog once swam too close to Big Black's home and nearly lost his life. If it hadn't been for the large snake meandering through at the time, it would have been curtains for our frog.

Big Black loved to snack on snakes, and for this reason everyone at Clay Pond enjoyed having him around. Our big fish was never a bother as long as all kept a safe distance.

In another part of the pond a young female bass was nearly hooked by a visiting fisherman. Big Black grabbed the line and hauled it into his own tangle of weeds. All our fisherman got that day was a hook full of duck weeds and an old boot for all his trouble.

Big Black kept a close eye on this young female fish. This was a good thing that served to divert his attention from all of the other pond residents. He was obviously 'love struck' as the eyes of the large bass glowed red whenever he was around the younger she-bass. Her eyes in turn twinkled as she saw him also. Our big bass will be busy now for a while, swooning over his new friend. You might say he had 'bigger fish to fry' than any of us. We were safe for now.

BONUS FISH TALE

From a fish's perspective.

Reel Fishing

Art and story piece by Don Ford

As a fish in the water we become nearly transparent. As long as we didn't move in the water, they couldn't see us. But we watched from below as angler after sordid fisherman noisily approached the stream, and clumsily tossed their worm and clunky sinker into the water. They actually thought the bright red and white bobber was going to attract us. Ha, Ha.

I once recalled a fisherman coming to our small brook and setting up a chair. Then he tossed his line in the water, while he sang some awful song that was extremely off key. I guess he liked to hear himself sing. His music, if that's what you want to call it, couldn't even attract a mosquito to bite, much less any of us fish.

Most sportsmen credit us with slyness and cunning; able to easily outsmart them. I like that! The truth is, we are very shy and spook easily. I guess they assume we are smart because we travel in schools.

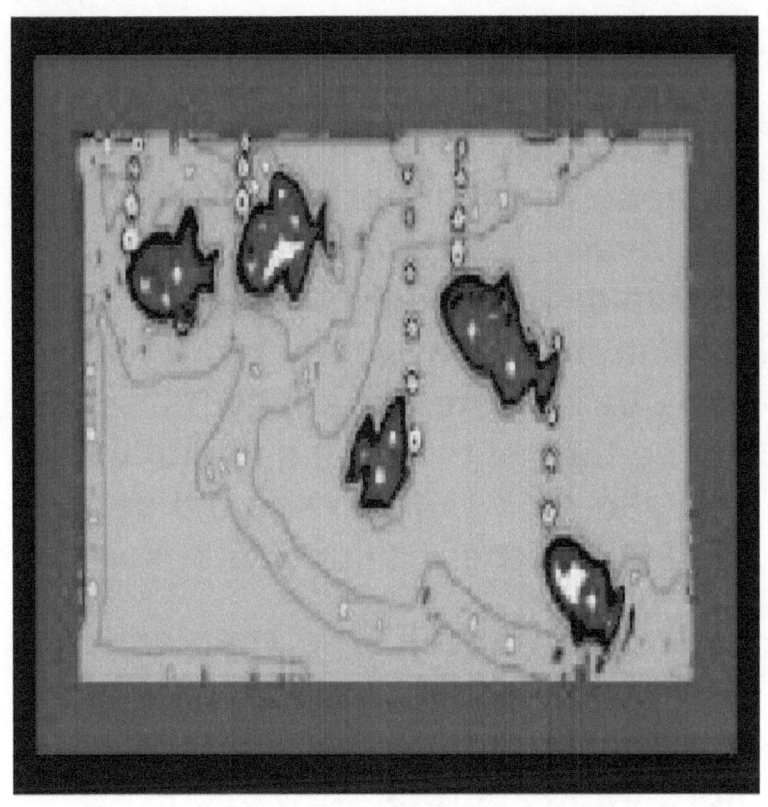

I absolutely love opening day of fishing. What a riot! I laugh my gills off most times. These clever sports enthusiasts, a little too enthused if you ask me, will line the shore of the stream. Ten or more join in a close row; side by side and almost touching. All of my friends in the water are chuckling too.

Most of these fish-hungry folks don't have a clue what we are hungry for. We are aware of the times and seasons and that certain foods are only available at precise time intervals. Those fishermen follow a set pattern. Always they bring the same bait; worms or salted minnows. Maybe they should eat a few of their own slimy worms and see if they would want them all the time. Yuck!

They should use a little imagination. How about tossing us a grasshopper or a cricket once in a while? Okay, no more trade secrets. Now each fisherman is on his or her own. I am not afraid of the average fisherman, but those veterans out there scare the scales right off me.

Life's most precious resource may
be leaving us.

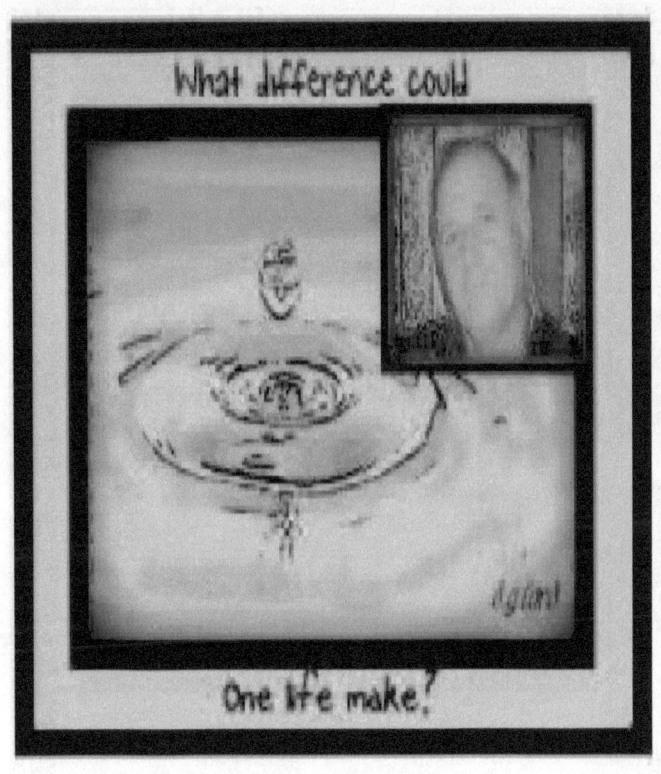

**Our Water Supply
Once Gone - It's Gone
Forever**

Water cascades over the brink

Falling, spilling endlessly

No effort expended in the fall

Always leaving, not returning

Gone but followed on its heels

Behind itself more water comes

Continues on in moving cycles

Tumbling, rumbling sounds heard

Rising bubbles and foam churning

At the bottom briskly carried off

Can water run and last forever?

Will it always quench the thirst?

How we care for these cool waters

Well determines what's in store

Someday, soon, brooks are silent

Maybe no more streams and rivers

Gone the sound of water lapping

Will shorelines matter any more?

Can we shake the guilt and blame?

When waters never return again.

Author Notes

This is a free verse poem that is not meant to rhyme. Only time will tell how long before we use up this life giving flow. There are efforts under way to conserve this resource and to clean up the pollutants found in it.

But is there enough time left? We better all hope there is! It seems that time is never on our side.

SPECIAL Note: News arrived this morning. A lake near us is being reclaimed and is starting to look pretty good. This is great news, since this lake has been on the worst water environmental list for some time.

About The Large Mouth Bass -

Myth 1: Bass don't like the sunlight since they don't have eyelids and the sun is too bright and hurts their eyes.

Fact: While a bass's eyes are fixed and can't close, bright light doesn't affect their eyes.

Myth 2: Bass prefer water temperatures of 70 to 72 degrees Fahrenheit.

Fact: Largemouth bass prefer temperatures of 82 to 84 degrees Fahrenheit. This is their favorite temperature if available. However, bass do well from 39 to 90 degrees Fahrenheit.

Attention Ice Fishermen -
Myth 3: Bass don't feed when the water temperature is below 50F.

Fact: Bass eat less food in cold water, but they still feed. Remember ("bass do well from 39 to 90 degrees Fahrenheit.")

Myth 4: Move a fishing lure slowly in cold water, because bass are slow swimmers in the icy water.

Fact: It's a good idea to reel the lure in slowly, to attract a fish; but it's not because a bass isn't fast. Reel your

line in as fast as you can, a fish will always swim faster, even in colder water.

Myth 5: Bass feed when their stomach is empty.

Fact: Bass feed when they want to or when they are hungry, whichever comes first. Hunger has nothing to do with food in their stomach.

Myth 6: Bigger lures or bait always catch bigger bass.

Fact: Little lures can catch big bass and big lures sometimes catch little ones.

Myth 7: Largemouth bass grow quicker than smallmouth bass.

Fact: Largemouth grow bigger than smallmouth, but in waters that provide good food both grow the same at least up to 4 or 5 pounds.

The Salmon

This fish is very interesting. You won't find him in a pond. When it comes time to spawn and have its babies, it climbs steep waterfalls; it's incredible to watch. Bears will jump right into the falls and grab one of these for supper.

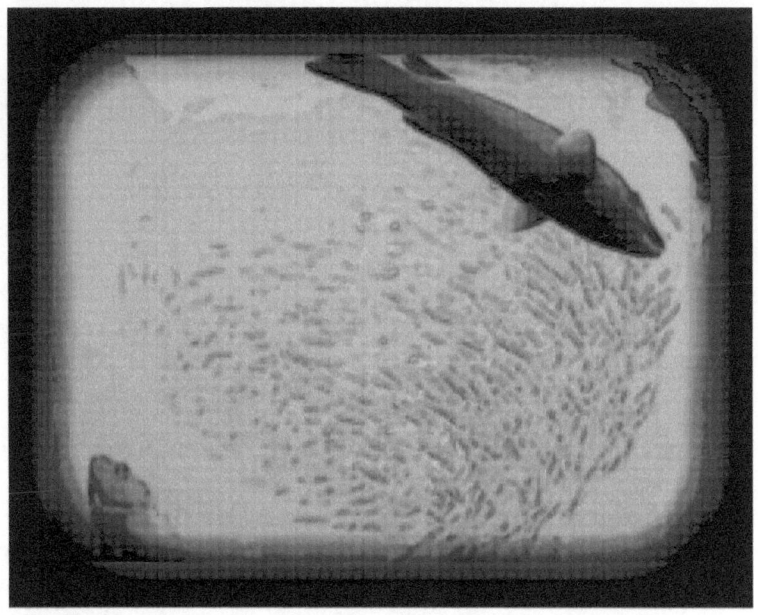

Fish travel in schools; that explains why they are all so smart and hard to catch!

The Urge to Spawn
by Don G. Ford

Talk about jumping through hoops
Watch salmon as they climb
Try swimming up stream yourself
They couldn't have chosen a worse time.

With a belly full of little ones
And trying to climb this hill
With the water rushing at them
They have this purpose to fulfill

Their babes will not be born here
At the bottom of this slide
So determined to reach the top
All obstacles are pushed aside

They risk a fall and maybe death
To reach a haven for their hatchlings
The urge to spawn; bring to birth
For salmon it's a generation thing

This tale a never-ending climb
Through the water they seem to fly
Year after enduring year they come
As with us things are hard in life

But in the end they reach their goal
Like the salmon, we can reach our heights
We know the best way is always up
There must be in each of us some *fight.

Note: Fight is the same as determination here. Like the salmon, we too will never give up, we will reach our goals too as we continue to climb with an end in sight.

Another great fish found in ponds is the Bullhead. Larger specimens of these are called Catfish and can grow to huge sizes, such as 4ft., 5ft., and 6ft. This particular fish breathes as we do, and so it can live out of water longer than most other fish. If you get one of these on your fishing line you will know it, as it is one of the best fighters in the water.

Held in High Esteem

Our story proceeds on from here. Clay Pond is home to a special insect, like the fish, it also eats smaller insects. See why we all love Lacy the dragonfly.

Ask anyone who has been attacked by a thirsty swarm of black flies, it will feel almost like an animal attack. They are like miniature vampires as they bite around your neck area like a feeding pool of Piranhas.

Fortunately for me, I was assisted at the very same time by an even more voracious and ferocious critter - out to eat them. The lone dragonfly came to my rescue, and in a matter of two minutes managed to fly all around my head and vanquish each and every one of my tormenters. This true story was published with Guidepost magazine, 2006 (Millions of readers).

P.S. If you see one of these beautiful iridescent insects in your backyard, thank her for me. REMEMBER: They eat the bugs that bug us! See Clay Pond Story "We all Love Lacy"

Clay Pond - We All Love Lacy
by Mr. Don G. Ford

DEAR LACY

When I was a small boy, and I would see you flying about, I wondered who you were. I asked my parents, and they said that you were like a Darning Needle. If any of us children were to talk too much, or ask too many questions, your job was to sew up our lips; we believed it. Did you think I talked too much as a kid? Excuse them, they didn't know the real you, like I do.

When I was in trouble, you were there. When I needed a friend to just be a friend, it was you. A few times you even made me laugh, along with those around me. You are good at lifting spirits with your acrobatic ways. Sometimes I wish you could hang around all year, but winter is just not your thing!

Today we will take you FISHING:

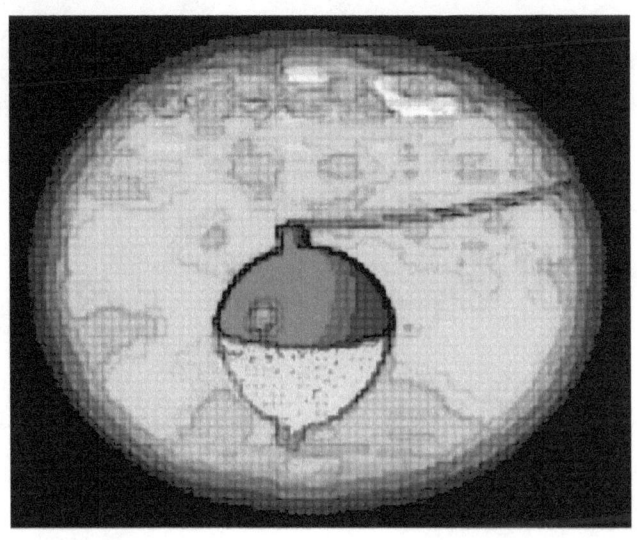

If this is your first time out, remember these simple rules.

Rule 1. Fish are very shy, so be quiet and move slowly as you head to the stream.

Rule 2. Never put more than one hook on your line. This is illegal.

Rule 3. Never ever let your hook show. Keep it covered with the bait at all times.

Rule 4. Don't throw stones in the water where you want to fish. This spooks the fish and they may not bite. Under the water, when the stone hits, it sounds like a firecracker going off to the fish.

Rule 5. Follow closely the limitations set on the amount of fish of different species you catch. This is usually a daily catch number. Also your state may have various times you are supposed to catch different types of fish.

Rule 6. Watch for signs near the fishing areas. Some may state you must catch and release anything on your line.

Rule 7. If you do catch something undesirable, like a snapping turtle, cut your losses and cut your line. The hook will dissolve over time and won't hurt the turtle.

Rule 8. If the streams and brooks are running fast and look muddy after a recent rain, never try to fish.

Rule 9. The very best times to fish are at the crack of dawn as the sun comes up or at the end of the day, when shadows disappear and no longer are seen on the water.

Rule 10. Take different kinds of bait to fish with. Like us, fish enjoy a change in their food choices from time to time.

Sometimes they like a juicy worm, other times they want salted minnows, etc. These are sold at hardware and convenience stores. At a drug store I worked we had plenty of worms for sale.
Different days they liked different things. That's why we bring different choices of bait.

My Uncle is a trophy fisherman; he's won many contests for the biggest fish. He took me early to a stream one morning. After fishing a one-mile stretch of water, I caught one little fish.

My uncle checked to see what my fish had been eating. It was tiny baby pink crabs. The crabs were spawning and this was the only time this food would be available to the fish.

We went to the shallow end and lifted rocks, only to find dozens of crabs that were spawning. After filling our bait box with pink crabs, we fished the same mile of water again and caught 22 more fish.

Rule 11. If it lightly begins to rain, stick around. The fish will still bite. The rain will sometimes loosen the mud along the stream bank and worms will wash into the water. Fish know this and watch and wait for dinner.

Rule 12. If the water is moving fast, you can put your worm on the line and lay it on a leaf. Then place it in the water and watch it float downstream.

After it has gone about ten or twelve feet in the water, hold the line tight

and the worm will drift off of the leaf
and into the water.

The fish sees the worm gently fall
into the water and it tries to be the
first one on the scene to get it.

Something else my Uncle taught me
was to wrap a worm already on your
hook in a soft mud ball.

The line with the mud ball on it is
tossed out into the running water.
It falls to the bottom and the fast
moving water starts to wear away the
mud allowing the worm to poke its
head through.

As the worm wiggles on its way out
of the dirt, the fish see it as a worm
coming out of the stream bank. It
looks more natural to them, and they
start to fight over it.

Fish where you can be alone, not
with other fishermen all along the

bank. Many fishermen park their car near where they want to fish and stay there.

I like to park my vehicle, then move up or down stream to where no one is fishing and it's quiet. I once followed a stream 300 to 400 yards down from a bridge, where 14 other fishermen were standing along the bank, side by side.

When I returned from my own private area of fishing, I had my limit of fish for the day. None of them had any luck. (But we know mine wasn't luck!)

TIP 1: Small fish need cover to hide from enemies, but largemouth bass also spend most of their time hiding too. The more weed beds there are in a given pond, the more places a big bass can lurk. The smaller fish can't very well hide in

the same place can they? But that's how our bass also finds and feeds on them.

TIP 2: Deep, Shaded Banks: Man-made ponds are typically shallow at one end and deep alongside the dam. Many times, landowners allow the dams of those ponds to grow up, especially with overhanging trees and other brush. Those deep, shaded sides (6 to 20 feet, depending on the pond) provide shelter from summer heat and temporary cover when other debris in the water isn't available.

A TRUE FISH STORY

One beautiful day in the simmer, three of us decided to stay overnight in a tent near a beaver dam. We fished this dam for a couple of hours, but only caught a few smaller trout.

Were there bigger fish in this larger pond? I was about to find out! Just before nightfall is the best time to fish – refer to Rule #9. I was headed back to our tent as the sun was slowly going down. We had set the tent up near the water, and suddenly I saw a giant bird fly down and splash the water.

This eagle could see the large brown trout from the sky and swooped down, capturing it in his talons; making a swift get away into the air.

What a cool sight to see as this Bald Eagle was flying away with a fish nearly half his own size. So the answer was yes, there were giant fish in this pond!

My Uncle showed up very early the next morning (The other really good time to catch fish) and he had a big brown trout on his line.

He cooked it up for breakfast for all of us. We then spent the rest of the day fishing upstream from the dam, where there were two great pools of water with big fish in them we could easily see.

The fish could see us too by now and none of them went after our bait! If the fish is in sight, you may never be able to catch him. But, if you wait until the sun falls below the horizon, then the fish can't see you anymore. Now drop your line in the water!

OTHER CLAY POND BOOKS listed here.

Clay Pond - What is a Woodie?

Clay Pond and Other Fish Tails

Clay Pond - Freddie The Frog & Thaddeus Toad

Clay Pond - Lady Bugley

More books by this same author. See listing & description>
http://tinyurl.com/l4al233

Book Shelf 1

Book Shelf 2

www.ingramcontent.com/pod-product-compliance
Lightning Source LLC
Chambersburg PA
CBHW030548290526
45786CB00004B/1924